Matters of Opinion

D1540776

CELL PHONES

By
ANDREA NAKAYA

WITHDRAWN

NORWOOD HOUSE PRESS
CHICAGO, ILLINOIS

Norwood House Press
P.O. Box 316598
Chicago, Illinois 60631

For information regarding Norwood House Press, please visit our website at:
www.norwoodhousepress.com or call 866-565-2900.

PHOTO CREDITS: Cover: © wavebreakmedia/Shutterstock.com; © AP Images/Stephen
Brashear, 32; © Arenacreative/Dreamstime, 35; © eXpose/Shutterstock.com, 19; © Ian
Allenden/Dreamstime.com, 47; © Mary F. Calvert/Zuma Press/MCT via Getty Images,
45; © Maximus117/Dreamstime.com, 41; © Melinda Fauver/Dreamstime.com, 21;
© Monkey Business Images/Shutterstock.com, 43, 50; © nenetus/Shutterstock.com, 16;
© Ocusfocus/Dreamstime.com, 29; © Pressmaster/Shutterstock.com, 31; © Rashevskyi
Viacheslav/Shutterstock.com, 8; © Robert Kneschke/Dreamstime.com, 24; © Tmcnem/
Dreamstime.com, 10; © Shooting Star Studio/Shutterstock, 13; © Syda Productions/
Shutterstock.com, 37; © Wavebreakmedia Ltd/Dreamstime.com, 17; © Wrangler/
Dreamstime.com, 7

Note: Words that are **bolded** in the text are defined in the glossary.

Time

1973 ▸ Martin Cooper, the general manager of Motorola's communications systems division, makes the first public cell phone call. His phone weighs about 2.5 pounds (1 kg), and its battery allows 20 minutes of talk time.

1983 ▸ The first cell phone is offered for sale to the public. The Motorola Dynatac 8000X sells for $3,995.

1985 ▸ There are 340,213 cell phone subscribers in the United States, which is less than 1 percent of the population.

1992 ▸ A Canadian sends the first text message. The message says, "Merry Christmas."

1993 ▸ Technology company IBM releases the Simon Personal Communicator, the first smartphone. It has a stylus for writing on the screen, and can be used for email.

1997 ▸ The cell phone industry launches a campaign called "Safety—Your Most Important Call," to help educate people about the danger of using a cell phone while driving.

2002 ▸ The first cell phones with built-in cameras become available.

2007 ▸ Apple forever changes the way people use cell phones when it releases the iPhone. The iPhone combines a phone, music player, and computer into one device, and it has a touch screen.

2009 reSTART, the first treatment facility in the United States for addiction to cell phones and other digital technology, opens in Fall City, Washington.

2010 Researchers performing a study to assess the level of cell phone distraction by drivers shows that drivers will not look up from their phones to notice a clown riding on a unicycle passing by the car.

2011 The World Health Organization decides that more proof is needed before cell phone use can be determined to cause cancer.

2012 A research study in Sweden using 4,000 young adult participants concludes that heavy cell phone use causes stress, depression, and sleep problems.

2013 Research company Nielsen finds that 70 percent of US teens own smartphones.

2014 A survey taken by Pew Research Center finds that half of cell phone owners would find giving up their cell phones extremely difficult.

1 An Essential Part of Daily Life

Most people could not imagine life without the cell phone. Almost everyone has one. The typical American youth gets his or her first phone at about twelve years old, although many are even younger. By the time they are in their teens, about three quarters of young people have a cell phone. Among adults, 90 percent own one. These devices have become an essential part of society.

Useful Tools

People use their cell phones for much more than making calls. Most American cell phones are like hand-held computers, and people can download useful programs—called apps—onto them, and also use them to connect to the Internet.

People spend hours a day using these **versatile** little computers and become very attached to them. One

By the time they are teens, about three quarters of young people have cell phones.

study found that more than half of smartphone owners do not go longer than an hour without checking their phone, and that they feel panicked if they lose it. In 2012 *Time* magazine questioned thousands of people in the United States and other countries about how they use their cell phones. Almost a third said their phone is the first and last thing they look at every day. Many said that they even sleep with their phone next to them at night. Managing editor of *Time* Nancy Gibbs comments, "It is hard to think of any tool, any instrument, any object

An almost endless array of apps can be downloaded onto a smartphone.

in history with which so many developed so close a relationship so quickly as we have with our phones."[1]

Concerns About Cell Phones

How this close relationship with the cell phone affects people is controversial. Critics worry that many cell phone users miss out on spending face-to-face time with other people or other important activities, such as being outside or being active, because they are glued to their phones instead. Some researchers also say that relying on a cell phone can cause people to lose their ability to solve problems or think for themselves, or even cause health problems like cancer. However, others believe that

? Did You Know

Cell Phone Use May Change the Brain

Evidence suggests that when young people spend large amounts of time using cell phones, their brains are affected. Researchers have found that the brain does not fully mature until a person is about twenty-five years old. Until that time, everything a young person thinks about and does has an impact on the way the brain develops. The brain cells and connections that are used a lot become stronger, and those that are not used die off. In order to develop a healthy brain, young people need to engage in a variety of activities every day, including exercise, time with friends, and time in school. When young people spend most of their time focused on cell phones instead, they may not give their brains the variety of experiences they need to properly develop.

such fears are exaggerated. They argue that cell phones make life easier and better by helping people with their daily activities. The phones may also help relationships by making it easier for friends and family to connect with one another. Overall, they insist that society has nothing to fear from making the most of this remarkable technology.

Other people worry about how cell phones affect privacy. Phones create an electronic record of all the things they are used for, so when people use their phones as a daily planner or for searching the Internet, texting, or taking photos, all these activities are permanently recorded. The American Civil Liberties Union cautions, "Your cell phone is a window into your whole life, from who your friends are to where you go."[2] If that information is used in the wrong way, it could harm a person's privacy. However,

People can and do transmit a lot of sensitive and personal information on their cell phones.

despite this risk, most people continue to use their cell phones. Overall, most cell phone owners believe that the benefits their cell phone gives them outweigh the threat to their privacy.

Cell Phone Distraction

Whether cell phones really do threaten privacy or harm personal health and development is still widely debated. However the harm that can occur from cell phone distraction is well documented. When people focus on using their cell phones, it can be difficult to pay attention to other things that are happening around them. Sometimes this can be a problem. The most harmful type of cell phone distraction is driving while using a phone. Safe driving requires that a driver give his or her full attention to the task of driving, and cell phone use makes this impossible. The World Health Organization estimates that people who drive while using a cell phone are four times more likely to be involved in a car accident than those who do not. It warns, "Distracted driving is a serious and growing threat to road safety."[3]

Unfortunately, research shows that despite that danger many people do use their phones while driving, often with deadly results. This includes young people. In 2014 the Centers for Disease Control and Prevention (CDC) reported that about 40 percent of teens who drive say

Cell phone use while driving significantly increases the risk of being involved in a car accident.

that they have texted or emailed while driving. One tragic case of texting and driving occurred in Michigan in 2014. According to news reports, seventeen-year-old Jacob Freybler was driving home at night when he veered onto the wrong side of the road while texting. Freybler's father says, "His last words to the two people he was texting were four words long. That was enough time to get over the center line and hit somebody head on."[4] Freybler was pinned in the car and pronounced dead at the scene. He also injured the driver of the other vehicle.

There is also evidence that a growing number of young children are being injured because their parents are distracted by cell phones and not properly watching them. Rahul Rastogi, an emergency-room doctor in Oregon comments that people simply do not realize just how distracting their phones can be. He says, "We think we're multitasking and not really feeling like we are truly distracted. But in reality we are."[5]

A Look Inside This Book

Cell phones are a controversial technology. In this book, three issues will be covered in more detail: Is reliance on cell phones harmful to relationships? Are cell phones addictive? Should children be allowed to own cell phones? Each chapter ends with a section called **Examine the Opinions**, which highlights one argumentation technique used in the chapter. At the end of the book, readers can test their skills at writing their own essay based on the book's topic. Notes, glossary, a bibliography, and an index in the back provide additional resources.

2 Is Reliance on Cell Phones Harmful to Relationships?

Cell phone users often focus so much on their phones that they ignore the people right in front of them, and this harms relationships. It is very common for people to constantly check their phones, and read or send texts in the middle of conversations with others. Psychologist Sherry Turkle gives an example. She says, "I went to a dinner of a group of young people, constant, constant interruption. Everybody has a phone, phones are going off constantly, the average teenage girl is interrupted once every four or five minutes by an incoming or an outgoing text."[6] When friends ignore and interrupt one another like this, they can make each other feel unimportant.

Cell phones have become a common form of communication among young adults.

Parents Distracted

It is not just young people that interrupt one another to look at their phones. Young people often report that their parents ignore them because they are so caught up with their own cell phones. Psychologist Catherine Steiner-Adair interviewed more than one thousand young people for a book about digital technology, and she talks about how this treatment makes them feel. "One of the many things that absolutely knocked my socks off," she says, "was the consistency with which children—whether they were 4 or 8 or 18 or 24—talked about feeling exhausted and frustrated and sad or mad trying to get their parents' attention."[7]

Empty Conversation

Another way cell phone communication damages relationships is by discouraging meaningful conversations. To build a strong friendship, people need to take the time to really get to know one another, and the best way to do

Parents can become so involved with their cell phones that they ignore their children.

Cell Phone Users Are Losing Social Skills

Experts worry that because many young people choose to communicate by phone instead of in person, they are not learning important social skills. For example, when people talk in person they need to learn to read body language—such as eye contact, facial expressions, or fidgeting—as well as what is actually said. Melissa Ortega is a child psychologist. She reports that many of the young people she sees have difficulty making small talk or focusing on a full conversation. She explains, "They don't have as much experience doing it because they're not engaging in it ever." She worries that this will be harmful later in life when they need these skills for things such as job interviews.

Melissa Ortega, quoted in Katherine Bindley, "When Children Text All Day, What Happens to Their Social Skills?" *Huffington Post*, December 9, 2011. www.huffingtonpost.com.

this is in person. However a lot of young people say that they prefer to communicate through texts or social networks instead. Researchers have found that when young people talk through text messages or social networking posts, their conversations are usually much more brief and **superficial**; often only a sentence or a few words at a time. It is impossible to really get to know and understand somebody this way. University professor Jeffrey G. Parker insists, "These good, close relationships . . . are essential to allowing kids to develop poise and allowing kids to play with their emotions, express emotions, all the functions of support that go with adult relationships."[8]

Less Sense of Community

Critics also argue that because people spend so much time on their phones, they no longer share a strong sense of community with the people that live in their neighborhoods or cities. In order to develop that sense of community, people need to interact with their neighbors.

People prefer to communicate via texts or social media instead of face-to-face interaction.

However, in many places it has become rare for people to say hello or even look at one another when they are in public because they are so **immersed** in their phones. CNN writer Jack Cafferty comments, "Most of us spend our days walking around with our noses buried in our cell phones, Blackberrys, iPhones, etc. And while we're doing that, we're tuning out the people who are actually in the same room as us."[9] This lack of interaction among neighbors means that it is impossible for them to develop a strong sense of community.

But Not So Fast...

No: Cell Phone Use Helps Strengthen Relationships

Cell phones help young people build stronger relationships with friends and family because they make it far easier to keep in touch. If a person had to physically go and meet another person every time they wanted to talk with them, communication would take a lot of time. Instead, cell phones let friends quickly and easily talk

Cell phones have become an essential tool for keeping in contact with friends and family.

by text or online message. Group messages and public postings save even more time by letting a person talk with many other people at once. The result of such easy communication is that young people are much closer with their friends and family. For example, high school teacher Beth Cafferty says that her 15-year-old daughter keeps in touch with her friends through hundreds of texts every day. She says, "I actually think they're closer because they're more in contact with each other—anything that comes to my mind, I'm going to text you right away."[10]

Young People Connect More Often Because of Phones

Researchers have found that despite the use of cell phones, most young people still recognize the value of talking to friends in person. One survey found that about half prefer to communicate that way. The researchers say, "It is interesting that even today's teens see the value in being able to look a friend in the eye and make her laugh. Yes, texting is fast and easy, and they use it a lot, but, as one teen wrote, 'moments' only happen in person." The researchers found that for most teens, cell phones have not replaced face-to-face communication; instead they simply provide an additional way to keep in touch. This means that many young people are connecting with friends more often overall, and develop stronger friendships than they would without cell phones.

Quoted in Common Sense Media, "Social Media, Social Life: How Teens View Their Digital Lives," Summer 2012. www.commonsensemedia.org.

Cell phones are especially helpful for friends and family members who live in different cities or even different countries from one another. One woman explains, "Almost everyone—my mom and dad, my three siblings and I, and some of my nieces and nephews—have cell phones with cameras. We all live far apart, so we keep in touch by sending humorous and cute pictures of our kids, special occasions (like school plays), and what the weather looks like outside."[11]

More Communication with Parents

Cell phones also make relationships with parents stronger because they make it easier for young people to update their parents about where they are and what they are doing. Many parents say they have found that giving their children cell phones has improved communication. Shawn DuBravac from the Consumer Electronics Association explains, "Parents I've talked to generally love that their kids have cell phones because they can text them when maybe a call wouldn't work. . . . I know students will often send photos of reports or grades that they've gotten to their parents."[12]

Some parents also report that while their children might be uncomfortable talking to them about certain things in person, they may be able to do so in a cell

Cell phones allow people to send photos to others and to post them to social media sites, allowing people to stay in contact with one another.

phone conversation. Florida mother Karla Campos says that her ten-year-old son doesn't talk to her very much in person. "I see him and pass by and he just says 'Hi Mom,'" says Campos. However, she insists that her phone allows her to have conversations with her son that would not otherwise happen. She says, "When I have real conversation with him, it's on the phone, through Facebook."[13]

Helping Shy People Socialize

Cell phones also help young people who are shy or feel nervous talking to others. Many shy people find it much easier to talk by text or online message because they do not have to actually face another person, and they have more time to think about what they want to say. Author Susan Cain points out that most shy people still want to talk to others, but they just find it challenging. She says, "This is what the Internet offers: the chance to connect—but in measured doses and from behind a screen. . . . You have time to think before you speak. You can connect, one mind with another, freed from the distractions of social cues and pleasantries."[14]

In addition, communicating by cell phone helps shy people strengthen their social skills so that they eventually become more comfortable using them in person, too. Atlanta father Robert Wilson talks about how chatting with friends through Facebook has been helpful to his **introverted** 14-year-old son Evan. Wilson says, "It's helping him come out of his shell and develop social skills that he wasn't learning because he's so shy."[15]

Closing Arguments

Cell phones have become an essential part of society; however, experts continue to disagree about how this reliance affects relationships. Some people believe heavy cell phone use damages friendships and family relationships and destroys society's sense of community, while others insist cell phones actually make connections between people stronger. As society continues to rely on phones for an increasing number of activities, debate over this issue will continue.

Examine the Opinions

Emotional Appeal

In order to persuade readers to accept their arguments, writers sometimes use emotional appeal. This means that they include stories or language that elicit a strong emotional reaction to the topic. When a reader reacts with strong emotions, he or she may be more likely to agree with the author's point of view. In the first essay, the author uses this technique to support the argument that cell phone use can damage relationships. She describes how young people feel when they are ignored by cell-phone-using friends and parents. For example, one psychologist says they are often, "exhausted and frustrated and sad or mad." By using this emotional language, the author is encouraging readers to also feel these emotions of exhaustion, frustration, sadness, or anger when they think about the way people use their phones.

3 Are Cell Phones Addictive?

 Yes: Cell Phones Are Highly Addictive

Cell phones are so addictive that most people who own them cannot help checking them constantly, using them for hours every day, and even sleeping with them at night. In 2012 *Time* magazine questioned thousands of people in the United States and other countries about how much they used their phones. Most of the people they talked to said they could not go more than a day without their phone. One-third said that being without their phone for even a short amount of time made them feel anxious.

Feeling like an Addict

Phone addiction can be so strong that when people do not have their phones, they describe their feelings in the same way as a drug addict going through withdrawal. Medical student Derek Smith kept track of his cell phone use for a whole week as part of a news story for CNN.

For many people, cell phones have replaced other daily nighttime activities such as reading.

During that week, Smith realized that he was extremely attached to his phone and felt like it was almost a part of his body. He says that when he accidentally left home without it he became anxious and depressed. "My palms get sweaty, my heart races, I start biting my lip,"[16] he says. All he can think about is going home to get the phone. Many cell phone owners feel the same way. In one study of teens, about 40 percent said they would describe themselves as addicted to their cell phones.

A study of college students in Maryland showed that cell phone withdrawal feelings are so strong that some people simply cannot stay away from their phones.

A Chemical Process in the Brain Makes Phones Addictive

Researchers believe that one reason cell phones might be addictive is because they can cause a chemical change in the brain. The human brain produces a chemical called dopamine that results in a very pleasurable feeling. Certain things cause the brain to release extra dopamine, and because this feels so good, some people get addicted to whatever causes that dopamine release. Cell phones stimulate dopamine because they offer the promise of rewards; people never know when they might discover something rewarding on their phones. Hilarie Cash, cofounder of an Internet addiction recovery center explains, "I never know what the next tweet is going to be. Who's sent me an e-mail? . . . What's waiting for me?"

Hilarie Cash, quoted in Elizabeth Cohen, "Does Life Online Give You 'Popcorn Brain'?" *CNN*, June 23, 2011. www.cnn.com.

Teachers challenged 200 students to stop using cell phones and any other media for 24 hours, and then write about their experiences. Most students reported that they were miserable in those 24 hours, and many were unable to even complete the challenge. For example, one student said, "The fact that I was not able to communicate with anyone via technology was almost unbearable." Another said, "I couldn't take it anymore being in my room . . . alone . . . with nothing to occupy my mind so I gave up shortly after 5pm. I think I had a good run for about 19 hours and even that was torture."[17]

Fighting Addiction

Because cell phones are so addicting, some people report using creative strategies to separate themselves, or their friends and family, from their phones. A Texas company even sells a small wooden box designed for people to stash their phones in while they take a break. The inside of the box says, "1. Insert Phone. 2. Close Lid."

At restaurants some diners play the phone stack game to encourage everyone to ignore their phones and talk to one another instead.

and the cover says, "3. Be Present."[18] Mark Love, who created the box, says that it was instantly a big hit and that people all over the world wanted to buy one.

A Serious Problem

In some countries, cell phone addiction is believed to be such a serious problem that the government is taking action to reduce it. Programs such as the reSTART program have been introduced for those who need help to break their addiction. In South Korea, the government estimates that millions of people there are

The reSTART Internet Addiction Recovery Program in Fall City, Washington, offers a 45-day treatment program that helps people break their addiction.

so addicted to their smartphones that it affects their work and social lives. Lee Yun-soo is a high school student in South Korea. She says that she hates being addicted to her smartphone. "I keep asking myself: 'Why did I buy a smartphone?' Sometimes I stay up all night using Facebook and tweeting."[19] In order to reduce problems like this, the South Korean government now requires schools to teach special classes that help students learn to use their phones responsibly.

But Not So Fast

 No: Cell Phones Are Used Constantly Because They Are Such Valuable Tools

While most people do spend a lot of time using their cell phones, this does not mean they are addicted. Being addicted to something means that a person continues to use it even when it has a negative effect on his or her life. Addiction expert Allen Frances explains, "To be considered 'addicted,' you should be compulsively stuck doing something that is no longer fun, feels out of control, serves no useful purpose, and is certainly not worth the pain, costs, and harms."[20] Simply using a cell phone for hours a day and checking it all the time, as many people do, does not qualify as addiction. As a result, the medical community has not officially recognized cell phone addiction as a real medical condition.

In fact, researchers have found that while most people agree that they are very attached to their cell phones, they actually say that this attachment makes their lives better. For example, Seattle mother Kathleen Baker says, "I am happy to have the advantage of owning a smartphone. I can't imagine how I would juggle a crazy job, three kids/family obligations, and doctoral studies without it! I am a happy addict."[21]

A Valuable Tool

The real reason people rely on their phones so much is because cell phones are such useful tools. A phone provides information and entertainment, keeps people in touch with others, and helps organize the day. High school students in Pennsylvania were asked about their cell phones, and many insisted that their phones help them in so many ways that they could not imagine living without them. Hannah

Some people compare constant cell phone use to chemical addictions. Others disagree.

Porter explains, "A cell phone is a necessary component in a person's everyday life, especially teenagers. Without it, we'd all be impotent and lost." She says, "A cell phone is a teenager's social life, a flashlight, a help guide, a dictionary and so much more."[22]

Young people who cannot imagine life without a cell phone are often described as digital natives. These youth have grown up using phones from a very young age. For them, constant attachment to a cell phone does not mean addiction; instead it is simply a normal way of life. Psychologist Ira Hyman explains, "Teens and young adults are natives in the land of technology. They have grown up with cell phones and the Internet. Their social lives are tied up in these machines; they live across the Internet and airwaves."[23]

Impossible to Be Without

Because this is the way most young people live, many find that it is impossible to have a social life without a cell phone. Even teens that dislike cell phones are often forced to use them because this is how most of their

Phones Offer an Instant Source of Information

Cell phones allow people to instantly get information about almost anything. With a phone, a person can easily search for answers online or can ask hundreds of friends at once with an instant message. A huge variety of apps also provide information and help solve problems. This is one reason people so often turn to their phones. In 2010, a man was trapped in the rubble of a Haiti hotel after a large earthquake. He used tools and information from his cell phone to help him survive. First, he used a first-aid app to figure out what to do about the bleeding wounds on his head and leg. Then, because the app warned him that he might be in shock and should not to go to sleep, he set his phone's alarm to go off every twenty minutes to keep him awake. After being trapped for more than 60 hours, the man was finally rescued. He believes his phone was one of the reasons he stayed alive so long.

Teens often rely on their cell phones to socialize with friends.

friends communicate. Psychologist Turkle says that she has known teens that become sick of being so attached to their phones and try to stop using them, but they eventually find themselves back using their phones. She explains, "That is sort of where their social life is. . . . That's where they know where the parties are. . . . That's where they find out where things are happening."[24] Teens without a phone report that they are often left out or ignored by friends.

Another reason that young people often rely on their cell phones is because it can be the only way they are able to socialize with friends. Technology researcher Danah

Boyd has spent years studying young people. She reports, "Over and over, kids tell me that they'd rather get together in person."[25] However, she says that for many kids, that has become difficult because they have busy after-school schedules or live far away from their friends.

Closing Arguments

There is no doubt that many people become extremely attached to their cell phones. However, there is disagreement over why this happens and whether it is a cause for concern. Some people insist that cell phones are addictive and that this is a serious problem for society. Others contend that cell phone attachment makes life better and is nothing to worry about. This continues to be a controversial issue.

Examine the Opinions

Testimonials

The use of **testimonials** is a common argumentative technique. When an author quotes a well-known figure, study, or expert on a subject, he or she is using a testimonial to support an argument. In the first essay, the author argues that cell phone addiction is a serious problem. In order to support her argument, she provides a number of testimonials from young people about their addiction experiences. The stories of a medical student, college students in Maryland, and a high school student in South Korea all strengthen her argument that cell phone addiction is a serious problem because they show that numerous real people have struggled with this issue.

4 Should Children Be Allowed to Own Cell Phones?

Yes: Cell Phones Benefit Children

Cell phones keep young people safe by helping them stay in touch with their parents and making it easy to call for help in an emergency. Anita Gurian, an expert in child psychiatry, explains that cell phones benefit youth and their parents in many ways. She says, "Kids can let parents know where they are, when they need to be picked up, when they'll be late, and just generally what's happening. Parents can let children know if their plans change, whether they'll be late, and where to meet. In many ways, cell phones make life easier and safer."[26] In addition, most phones have a GPS tracking feature so that if a child ever gets lost, their parents can find them by using that feature to locate the child's phone.

Most cell phones have a built-in GPS tracking feature.

Misuse Is Not Common

While critics worry about young people being harmed by cell phone misuses such as bullying or sexting, a number of studies show that concerns about these problems have been exaggerated. Bullying can be a serious problem for young people. However, some research shows that bullying in person, not by cell phone,

Should Children Be Allowed to Own Cell Phones? **41**

is the real problem. Michele Ybarra, a public health researcher, carried out a study of about 1,600 young people and found that cell phones do not seem to have increased bullying among youth. Her study showed that when bullying does happen, it is usually in person, not by cell phone. Other studies show that sexting is also far less common than people think. In one survey of 1,560 young people, only about 2½ percent said they had ever sexted. The researchers concluded that sexting is not a common thing for young people to do.

Preparing for the Future

Cell phones also benefit youth by teaching them to be **fluent** in modern technology. Most people believe that cell phones and other digital technology will be essential to life in the future. The Pew Research Center interviewed a number of technology experts about their predictions for the future, asking them what types of skills they believe young people will need. Many replied that the networking and information-finding skills that young people practice on their phones today will help them be successful in the future.

Experts claim that cell phone use will help children be more successful in the future.

Experts insist that it is not realistic for parents to prevent their children from owning cell phones because they are afraid of the potential harms. Cell phones are such an important part of society that youth will be exposed to them eventually. Psychiatrist Dan Becker says, "We can't pretend youngsters won't use these tools." He points out that many things in life are potentially dangerous, but that does not mean they should not be used. For instance, he says, "Think about cars. Learning to drive is almost indispensable today, but cars can also be misused."[27] Instead, the best way to deal with the risks posed by cell phones is not to refuse to let youth use them, but to teach them how to use them safely.

A Tool for Learning

Not only are cell phones essential for young people's futures, but they can be powerful learning tools for the present. High school teacher Jamie Williams teaches

Cell Phones Help Youth Be Heard

When young people use their cell phones to send messages, they have the power to be heard by thousands, or even millions of other people. In the past, only the government or other powerful organizations such as television networks had the power to spread a message to a large number of people. Cell phones and the Internet have changed that. With a cell phone, young people can send messages that can be seen by all of their friends, who can pass it on to all of their friends, and so on. One youth's message can end up being viewed by people all over the world. This means that if a young person strongly believes in something and wants to tell others, he or she has the power to do so.

Teachers have begun incorporating cell phones into technology and art classes.

art and technology classes. He not only approves of students using their cell phones in his classes but actually makes them do so. A journalist describes Williams's classes. She says, "For his art class, he asks students to use photos they've taken on their cell phones as the basis for paintings they'll create. . . . In his video class, most students have phones capable of shooting in high definition, and use them for projects."[28]

But Not So Fast...

Cell phones put young people in danger by **facilitating** harmful behavior. A cell phone is a powerful tool that needs to be used responsibly, and many young people are not mature enough to do so. Author Liz Perle warns that a cell phone gives a young person a huge amount of power. She says, "When you hand kids phones today, you're giving them powerful communications and production tools. They can create text, images, and videos that can be widely distributed and uploaded to Web sites. They can broadcast their status and their location. They can download just about everything in the world."[29] Many young people are not mature enough to be given this much freedom, and when they have it they often behave inappropriately. For example, it is common for young people to use their phones to share information or pictures that they later regret, or even to do things that they know are wrong, such as bullying other people.

Cell phones provide young people with large amounts of power. How they choose to use this power is up to them.

Bullying

Bullying is a serious problem among young people that can cause lasting emotional harm. Some research shows that young people use their phones to bully others by using texts or other online messages. The website *Bullying Statistics* says that approximately one in five teens will be bullied by text. It explains that bullying that happens by phone can be even more harmful than face-to-face bullying for a number of reasons:

- It can happen 24 hours a day, even at home, which is usually a refuge from bullying, so it can feel inescapable.
- Text bullies are often much meaner because they don't have to see their victims.
- The victims may not know who is sending the messages, which can be frightening.[30]

Sexting

Cell phones have also led to the practice of sexting, which can be just as harmful as bullying. When sexting, young people send or receive sexually explicit photos or videos. Many researchers believe that as cell phone use among young people has become more common, so has sexting. One survey of almost 1,200 middle school students in Los Angeles revealed that about 1 in 5 had received a sexually explicit message or photo of somebody. While a young person might intend for a sext

Cell Phones Reduce Time for Reflection

Psychologists believe that it is very important for young people to have periods of downtime so that they can learn how to be alone and how to entertain themselves. Downtime also gives them the opportunity to process and reflect on things that have happened to them throughout the day. All of this is thought to be an important part of normal development and well-being. However, when young people remain constantly engaged with their cell phones—texting or playing games whenever they become bored—they are missing out on this downtime. David Greenfield, founder of the Center for Internet and Technology Addiction says, "People have lost the ability to sit in nothingness even for a moment." Experts worry that without time to reflect and to be alone, young people will not become happy, well-rounded adults.

David Greenfield, quoted in Beth Kassab, "Are You Addicted to Your Smartphone?" *Orlando (FL) Sentinel*, November 25, 2013. http://articles .orlandosentinel.com

to be viewed only by the person it was sent to, in reality these messages are often shared with other people and can cause teasing, bullying, and great harm to a young person's feelings and reputation.

Many young people take their phones everywhere for fear of missing out on texts or emails.

Physical Harm

In addition to causing harm through bullying or sexting, cell phones can also be bad for young people's health. Researchers have found that people who spend a lot of time using their phones are more likely to feel stressed. This is because they often feel like they need to constantly check their phones in order to know what their friends are doing. Columnist Beth Kassab explains that this is very stressful. She says, "People aren't wired to be in a constant state of alertness. That keeps levels of stress hormones high and might eventually hurt how well you sleep or even take a toll on your heart."[31]

Closing Arguments

It is becoming increasingly common for even young children to have their own cell phones. However, there is disagreement over whether cell phones are actually appropriate or safe for children. Some people insist that the phones are not only appropriate but greatly beneficial. Others caution that when children have cell phones, they may be harmed or tempted to engage in harmful behavior. This remains an important issue.

Examine the Opinions

Statistical Evidence

One way to make a strong argument is to provide **statistical evidence**. Statistics are numerical data, and they often come from researchers who have studied and analyzed large numbers of cases in order to discover patterns. Both these essays contain statistical evidence about bullying and sexting via cell phones. In the first essay, the author cites two different studies—each involving more than a thousand youth—to support her argument that neither bullying nor sexting are common. The second essay also contains statistics about these activities; however, this data supports the opposite argument—that sexting and bullying are actually quite common.

As this shows, while statistics can be persuasive, readers need to remember that different researchers may make different conclusions and that conflicting statistics often exist. It is thus important to thoroughly research an issue and look at different points of view before coming to any conclusions about that issue.

Write Your Own Essay

In this book, the author gave many opinions about cell phones. These opinions can be used to write a short essay on cell phones. Short opinion essays are a common writing form. They are also a good way to use the ideas in this book. The author gave several common argumentative techniques and evidence that can be used. Emotional appeal, testimonials, and statistical evidence were argumentative techniques used in the essays to sway the reader. Any of these could be used in a piece of writing.

There are 6 steps to follow when writing an essay:

Step One: Choose a Topic

When writing your essay, first choose a topic. You can start with one of the three chapter questions from the table of contents in this book.

Step Two: Choose Your Theme

Decide which side of the issue you will take. After choosing your topic, use the materials in this book to write the thesis, or theme, of your essay. You can use the titles of the articles in this book or the sidebar titles as examples of themes. The first paragraph should state your theme. For example, in an essay titled "Texting Is the Best Way to Communicate with Friends," state your opinion. Say why you think texting is the best way for friends to keep in touch with one another. You could also use a short anecdote, or story, that proves your point and will interest your reader.

Step Three: Research Your Topic

You will need to do some further research to find enough material for your topic. You can find useful books and articles to look up in the bibliography and the notes of this book. Be sure to cite your sources, using the notes at the back of this book, as an example.

Step Four: The Body of the Essay

In the next three paragraphs, develop this theme. To develop your essay, come up with three reasons why texting is a good way to communicate. For example, three reasons could be:

- *Because texting is so quick and easy, people can keep in touch with more friends at once.*
- *Friends cannot always physically be together, but texting allows them to communicate even when they are apart.*
- *Texting can make friendships stronger because they make it easier for people to share experiences they might be too shy to discuss in person.*

These three ideas should each be given their own paragraph. Be sure to give a piece of evidence in each paragraph. This could be a testimonial from a young person whose social life has improved since he or she got a cell phone. It could be a story or language with emotional appeal; for instance a young person describing how happy he or she feels after texting with friends that live far away. You could also use statistical evidence to convince your reader. An example of this would be to find a survey that shows that the majority of people say they have stronger friendships because of texting. Each paragraph should end with a transition sentence that sums up the main idea in the paragraph and moves the reader to the next one.

Step Five: Write the Conclusion

The final, or fifth, paragraph should state your conclusion. This should restate your theme and sum up the ideas in your essay. It could also end with an engaging quote or piece of evidence that wraps up your essay.

Step Six: Review Your Work

Finally, be sure to reread your essay. Does it have quotes, facts, and/or anecdotes to support the conclusions? Are the ideas clearly presented? Have another reader take a look at it to see whether someone else can understand your ideas. Make any changes that you think can help make your essay better.

Congratulations on using the ideas in this book to write a personal essay!

Chapter 1: An Essential Part of Daily Life

1. Nancy Gibbs, "Your Life Is Fully Mobile," *Time*, August 16, 2012. http://techland.time.com.

2. American Civil Liberties Union, "Cell Phones," no date. https://www.dotrights.org/cell-phones

3. World Health Organization, "Mobile Phone Use: A Growing Problem of Driver Distraction," 2011. http://www.who.int.

4. Jim Freybler, quoted in Troy Campbell, "Father of Killed Teen Warns of Texting While Driving Danger," Fox 17 News, September 29, 2014. http://fox17online.com.

5. Rahul Rastogi, quoted in Ben Worthen, "The Perils of Texting While Parenting," *Wall Street Journal*, September 29, 2012. http://www.wsj.com.

Chapter 2: Is Reliance on Cell Phones Harmful to Relationships?

6. Sherry Turkle, interviewed by Bill Moyers, "Segment: Sherry Turkle on Being Alone Together," *Moyers & Company*, October 18, 2013. http://billmoyers.com.

7. Catherine Steiner-Adair, quoted in Steve Henn, "When Parents Are the Ones Too Distracted by Devices," NPR, April 16, 2014. www.npr.org.

8. Jeffrey G. Parker, quoted in Hilary Stout, "Antisocial Networking?" *New York Times*, April 30, 2010. www.nytimes.com.

9. Jack Cafferty, "Technology Replacing Personal Interactions at What Cost?" CNN, January 3, 2011. http://caffertyfile.blogs.cnn.com.

10. Beth Cafferty, quoted in Stout, "Antisocial Networking?" www.nytimes.com.

11. Andrea Keeshan, answer to, "How Do You Stay Connected to Those You Love?" Real Simple, no date. www.realsimple.com.

12. Shawn DuBravac, quoted in Lindsey Boerma, "Kids with Cell Phones: How Young Is Too Young?" CBS News, September 2, 2014. www.cbsnews.com.

13. Carla Kampos, quoted in Adam Kuperstein, "Cell Phone Addiction Fuels Fear," NBC Miami, May 8, 2012. www.nbcmiami.com.

14. Susan Cain, quoted in Maia Szalavitz, "How Texting and IM-ing Helps Introverted Teens," *Time*, August 30, 2012. http://healthland.time.com

15. Robert Wilson, quoted in Stout, "Antisocial Networking?" www.nytimes.com.

Chapter 3: Are Cell Phones Addictive?

16. Derek Smith, quoted in Brandon Griggs, "800 Texts in One Week? Diaries of 3 Smartphone Addicts," CNN, October 9, 2012. www.cnn.com.

17. Quoted in A Day Without Media, "2. Feelings About Media," 2010. http://withoutmedia.wordpress.com.

18. www.bepresentbox.com/contact.html.com.

19. Lee Yun-soo, quoted in In-Soo Nam, "A Rising Addiction Among Youths: Smartphones," *Wall Street Journal*, July 20, 2013. online.wsj.com

20. Allen Frances, "Internet Addiction: The Next New Fad Diagnosis," *Huffington Post*, October 31, 2012. www.huffingtonpost.com.

21. Kathleen Baker, quoted in Brandon Griggs, "800 Texts in One Week?" www.cnn.com.

22. Hannah Porter, quoted in *Northeast Times*, "Can You Imagine Life Without a Cell Phone?" June 19, 2013. www.northeasttimes.com.

23. Ira Hyman, "Are You Addicted to Your Cell Phone?" *Psychology Today*, March 27, 2013. www.psychologytoday.com.

24. Sherry Turkle, interviewed by Bill Moyers. http://billmoyers.com.

25. Danah Boyd, quoted in Dalton Conley, "Wired for Distraction: Kids and Social Media," *Time*, March 19, 2011. http://content.time.com.

Chapter 4: Should Children Be Allowed to Own Cell Phones?

26. Anita Gurian, "Kids and Cell Phones: Staying Connected," Child Study Center, no date. http://www.aboutourkids.org.

27. Dan Becker, quoted in Sutter Health, Mills-Peninsula Health Services, "Teens, Computer Addiction and Mental Health," no date. http://www.mills-peninsula.org.

28. Audrey Watters, "Why Schools Should Stop Banning Cell Phones, and Use Them for Learning," PBS, August 29, 2011. http://www.pbs.org

29. Liz Perle, "When Should You Get Your Kid a Cell Phone?" PBS, 2010. http://www.pbs.org.

30. Bullying Statistics, "Text Bullying," no date. http://www.bullyingstatistics.org.

31. Beth Kassab, "Are You Addicted to Your Smartphone?" http://articles.orlandosentinel.com.

etiquette: Proper manners and rules that people are expected to follow when they interact with others.

facilitating: Making something easier.

fluent: To have a good understanding of something.

immersed: To be deeply involved in something.

introverted: Describes a shy person who finds it easier to be alone than in social situations with other people.

statistical evidence: A piece of numerical data.

superficial: Only focusing on the surface of something and never getting a true understanding of it.

testimonial: A statement made by another person that supports an argument.

versatile: Useful in many different ways.

Books

Sandra Donovan, *Communication Smarts: How to Express Yourself Best in Conversations, Texts, E-mails, and More.* Minneapolis: Twenty-First Century Books, 2013.

Debra Fine, *Beyond Texting: The Fine Art of Face-to-Face Communication for Teenagers.* New York: Canon, 2014.

Articles

Katherine Bindley, "When Children Text All Day, What Happens to Their Social Skills?" *Huffington Post*, December 9, 2011. www.huffing tonpost.com.

Naomi Canton, "Cell Phone Culture: How Cultural Differences Affect Mobile Use," CNN, September 28, 2012. www.cnn.com.

Common Sense Media, "Social Media, Social Life: How Teens View Their Digital Lives," Summer 2012. www.commonsensemedia.org.

Tony DeAngellis, "Is Technology Ruining Our Kids?" American Psychological Association, October 2011. www.apa.org.

Federal Communications Commission, "The Dangers of Texting While Driving," December 8, 2014. www.fcc.gov.

Brandon Griggs, "800 Texts in One Week? Diaries of 3 Smartphone Addicts," CNN, October 9, 2012. www.cnn.com.

Ira Hyman, "Are You Addicted to Your Cell Phone?" *Psychology Today*, March 27, 2013. www.psychologytoday.com.

Joanna Moorhead, "Why We Shouldn't Worry About Teenagers Using Mobile Phones," *Guardian* (Manchester, UK), May 20, 2014. www.theguardian.com.

Maia Szalavitz, "How Texting and IMing Helps Introverted Teens," *Time*, August 30, 2012. http://healthland.time.com.

Websites

SafeKids.com (www.safekids.com/cell-phone-safety-tips/). SafeKids contains important safety tips for youth about cell phone use.

NetSmartz Workshop (www.netsmartz.org /NSTeens). This website has six short videos that teach important safety concepts for cell phones and other technology.

About the Author

Andrea C. Nakaya, a native of New Zealand, holds a BA in English and an MA in communications from San Diego State University. She has written and edited more than thirty-five books on current issues. She currently lives in Encinitas, California, with her husband and their two children, Natalie and Shane.